CONTEMPORARY LIVES

EMMA STONE

BREAKOUT MOVIE STAR

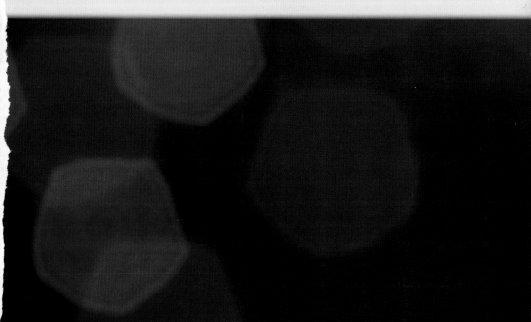

ABDO
Publishing Company

EMMA STONE

BREAKOUT MOVIE STAR

by Lisa Owings

CREDITS

Published by ABDO Publishing Company, PO Box 398166, Minneapolis,
MN 55439. Copyright © 2014 by Abdo Consulting Group, Inc. International
copyrights reserved in all countries. No part of this book may be reproduced in
any form without written permission from the publisher. The Essential Library™
is a trademark and logo of ABDO Publishing Company.

Printed in the United States of America,
North Mankato, Minnesota
102013
012014

 THIS BOOK CONTAINS AT LEAST 10% RECYCLED MATERIALS.

Editor: Angela Wiechmann
Series Designer: Emily Love

Photo credits: Shutterstock Images, cover, 3, 12, 31, 48, 67, 96, 97 (top);
Columbia Pictures/Everett Collection, 6, 34, 42; Jeremy Cowart/20th Century
Fox Film Corp./Everett Collection, 11; cinemafestival/Shutterstock Images, 14,
100; Seth Poppel/Yearbook Library, 18, 23; John Shearer/Invision/AP Images,
24; Marcocchi Giulio/SIPA/Newscom, 32; Fox Atomic/20th Century Fox/
Everett Collection, 39; Kiley Bishop/London Ent/Splash/Newscom, 44; Columbia
Pictures/Album/Newscom, 54, 78; Adam Taylor/Screen Gems/Everett Collection,
56; Screen Gems/Album/Newscom, 60; Featureflash/Shutterstock Images, 63,
97 (bottom); Matt Sayles/AP Images, 68, 98; Debby Wong/Shutterstock Images,
73; Rex Features/AP Images, 75, 99 (top); KGC-42/starmaxinc.com/Newscom,
83; Featureflash/Shutterstock Images, 87, 99 (bottom); Joe Klamar/AFP/Getty
Images/Newscom, 88; Wilson Webb/Warner Bros./Everett Collection, 91; Kristin
Callahan/Everett Collection, 94

Library of Congress Control Number: 2013946065

Cataloging-in-Publication Data

Owings, Lisa.
 Emma Stone: breakout movie star / Lisa Owings.
   p. cm. -- (Contemporary lives)
Includes bibliographical references and index.
ISBN 978-1-62403-228-8
1. Stone, Emma, 1988- --Juvenile literature. 2. Actors--United States--Biography-
-Juvenile literature. 3. Singers--United States-- Biography--Juvenile literature. 1.
Title.
791.4302/8092--dc23
[B]

                                                          2013946065

CONTENTS

Emma Stone tried to get a start in Hollywood for years before her big break in *Superbad*.

CHAPTER 1

Up from Rock Bottom

||||||||||||||||||||||||||||||||||||||||||||

Emma Stone had a rough start in Hollywood. By 2006, the 18-year-old had spent three years auditioning for nearly every television show with a character her age. But she had yet to be cast in anything other than a few guest appearances and canceled shows. She was getting frustrated with the rejections and disappointments.

Finally, Stone found the role she thought would make her a star. She began the audition process for the character of Claire Bennet, a courageous cheerleader with self-healing superpowers, on the NBC show *Heroes*. Auditions went well, and things were looking up.

In the final round of auditions, Stone was one of a few candidates still vying for the part. She waited outside the casting room for her turn to audition. She tried listening in on the conversation inside the room as another young woman was auditioning. What she overheard was devastating. Stone later recalled:

> *I could hear that, in the other room, a girl had just gone in and they were saying, "You are our pick. . . . On a scale of one to ten, you're an eleven."*[1]

Moments later, blonde starlet Hayden Panettiere breezed out of the room. "As I passed her, I knew she had the part," Stone said.[2] Indeed, Panettiere went on to star in the series.

That meant yet another rejection for Stone. She took a deep breath and went through with her audition, fully knowing it was pointless. It was one of the most difficult moments of her career.

> **"You have to believe, as an actor, if you didn't get a part that you really, really wanted and it went to someone else, it was because it was theirs to begin with."**[4]
>
> —*EMMA STONE*

When Stone got home, she was overwhelmed by emotion. An unbearable sense of failure descended on her. She had convinced her parents to let her move to Los Angeles, California, because she was determined to be a successful actor. But after three years and countless auditions, it hadn't happened. Now she was almost convinced it never would.

FROM DISAPPOINTMENT TO OPPORTUNITY

Stone described her failed *Heroes* audition as "rock bottom."[3] Still, she wasn't ready to give up. It might have been a huge disappointment, but it was also an opportunity. With nothing to lose and nowhere to go but up, she no longer had any excuse to hold her back in pursuit of her dream.

Over the next couple weeks, Stone went on more auditions. She put everything she had into her performances. Stone was cast as sassy teenager Violet Trimble in the FOX action series *Drive,* set to air in the spring of 2007. She was happy to get the part, especially because Violet was a permanent character. Although the show would ultimately be canceled after only four episodes, landing the role was a small success for Stone. It meant her luck was changing.

SUPERBAD

Stone hoped that luck would hold for an opportunity she was even more excited about. When the script for the big-screen teen comedy *Superbad* fell into Stone's hands in 2007, it was love at first read. She thought it was hilarious. She said, "It's completely my sense of humor, so I was like, 'Finally! A script that gets me!'"[5] Stone was determined to audition for the role of Jules, the attractive yet approachable hostess of a high school party. Even though the film was not yet approved for production, she jumped at the chance to be a part of something so true to her style of comedy.

Stone landed a role as Violet Trimble on *Drive*, a short-lived television series.

Stone tried her best to demonstrate her comedic talent at the audition. She got to show off her improvisation skills with fellow comic actor Jonah Hill, whose character, Seth, has a major crush on Jules. The fact that Stone could easily make up funny lines on the spot was impressive, but she didn't see it that way at the time. "I didn't think my audition was all that great," she later said.[6]

Audiences loved Stone's character—and red hair—when
Superbad launched her career.

Luckily, Judd Apatow, the film's producer,
thought otherwise. He cast her in the film with one
request: that she dye her blonde hair red. Stone

Judd Apatow is a screenwriter, director, and producer. He is best known for directing raunchy comedies, including *The 40-Year-Old Virgin* (2005) and *Knocked Up* (2007). One of his first claims to fame was as the executive producer of the 1999–2000 cult favorite *Freaks and Geeks* on NBC. In addition to producing *Superbad*, he also produced the 2011 movie *Bridesmaids*, among other comedy hits. Stone feels she owes everything to Apatow for her start in Hollywood. "I think without [*Superbad*], most of this [success] probably wouldn't have occurred," she said.[7]

did. And just like that, she was on her way to the big screen—and the breakthrough role she had been waiting for.

When *Superbad* came out in 2007, audiences fell in love with Jules right along with Seth. Stone came across as mature, compassionate, and witty. Although she didn't have a starring role in the movie, Stone's performance made a big impression—the kind of impression that would jump-start her career.

||||||||||

Born Emily Jean Stone, the star knew at a young age she was destined for Hollywood.

CHAPTER 2
Aspiring Star

||||||||||||||||||||||||||||||||||||||||||||||||||||||||||||||||||||||||||||||||||||||

Emily Jean Stone came into the world on November 6, 1988. Her parents, Krista and Jeff Stone, lived in Scottsdale, Arizona. Jeff owned a general-contracting company, while Krista was a homemaker. Krista often called her daughter Emma as a nickname—and it would eventually become Emily's stage name.

The early days of Emily's life were not quite what her parents had envisioned. For the first six months,

A hiatal hernia occurs when part of the stomach pushes up through the diaphragm muscle into the chest. Normally, the diaphragm squeezes around the esophagus—the tube that connects the mouth to the stomach. This squeezing generally keeps stomach acid from coming up into the esophagus. In people with a hiatal hernia, however, the diaphragm muscle squeezes around the upper part of the stomach instead. That means it is easier for stomach acid to enter the esophagus. This can cause painful heartburn, difficulty swallowing, and other issues. This discomfort caused Emily to cry and scream constantly as a baby.

Emily screamed—constantly. Her parents learned she had been born with a hiatal hernia, a condition with painful stomachaches that caused Emily to cry for hours on end. "To this day, my mom is sent into violent shudders if she hears a baby crying like that!" she exclaimed in a 2012 interview.[1] The nonstop crying damaged Emily's vocal chords before she could even talk. It created the deep, smoky voice she's now known for.

As Emily grew older, the crying stopped. In time, her true personality began shining through. She was loud, and she liked to boss other kids around. She had a flair for over-the-top theatrics. One of her favorite activities was putting on impromptu plays with her friends. Instead of trying to tone down Emily's bold personality, her parents nurtured their daughter's individuality.

Her parents also shared their love of comedy with her at an early age. Before she was even eight years old, her father had introduced her to his favorite comedies—many of which were too raunchy or mature for most children. They enjoyed such movies as the 1978 classic *Animal House* and 1987 favorite *Planes, Trains and Automobiles*. They also loved *The Jerk*, a 1979 comedy starring Steve Martin. The movie made a huge impression on Emily and is still one of her favorites. Young Emily wanted to make people laugh, as Martin did. She later recalled of the movies, "I loved them and my dad loved them, and we would laugh together, and I would think, 'This is love.' I just wanted to make people feel like that."[2]

Krista also helped shape the youngster's comedic tastes. Krista and Emily often watched the sketch comedy show *Saturday Night Live* (*SNL*). The two especially enjoyed classic sketches from the late 1970s and early 1980s. Emily's favorite

Young Emily had a love for comedy and a flair for theatrics.

cast member was Gilda Radner, who was known for her colorful characters and hilarious celebrity impersonations. Radner was a major inspiration for Emily to become a comedian.

ACTING OUT

Emily attended Sequoya Elementary in Scottsdale. Those early school days should have been fun and carefree, but Emily was plagued by constant anxiety. She had her first panic attack when she was just eight years old. After that, Emily sought comfort in her mother, trying to be at her side at all times. This meant going to school was difficult because it separated her from her mother. "I was just kind of immobilized by [anxiety]," she said of that time. "I didn't want to go to my friends' houses or hang out with anybody, and nobody really understood."[3]

EMILY'S ANXIETY

Emily was burdened by anxiety as a child. As an adult, she has never revealed whether her childhood anxiety stemmed from a specific event. However, in an interview with director and screenwriter Cameron Crowe, she admitted she experienced something traumatic when she was six years old—even before she began suffering from anxiety. She chose to keep the details of the event private, but she confessed that experience had come back to haunt her throughout her life. "It's the thing that I return to when I'm making a decision out of fear. Anything that I'm doing out of fear is defined by that moment," she said.[4]

Emily's parents were understandably concerned. They enrolled her in therapy, but Emily's struggles with anxiety continued for roughly two years. It was not until age 11 that she found a healthy way to cope with her fears—she discovered acting.

Krista took Emily to acting classes. Emily enjoyed them, and she soon began auditioning for plays at the Valley Youth Theatre in Phoenix, Arizona. She became a regular performer, playing Tweedledum in *Alice in Wonderland* and Eeyore in *A Winnie-the-Pooh Christmas Tail*. She also played roles in *The Little Mermaid*, *The Princess and the Pea*, and more.

Emily's natural talent for comedy impressed the staff at the youth theater. They invited her to join the theater's improvisational comedy troupe. She agreed, and the decision changed her life.

Through improv, Emily learned how to deal with uncertainties and overcome challenges. She learned how to think quickly. And she learned it was okay to take risks, because if you failed at something in improv comedy, you could just tell another joke. "Improv was my sport," she said,

Emily's parents placed a lot of trust in her. They allowed her to do just about anything she wanted so long as she didn't abuse that trust. While some adolescents rebel against strict parents, Emily had no need to rebel. "Since everything was allowed, it made me not want to do crazy [stuff]," she said.[6] She also explained how her parents' permissiveness made it difficult for her to lie to or keep secrets from them.

Once when she was 13 years old, some friends stopped by her house in the middle of the night. They wanted her to sneak out for a late-night candy run. But Emily wouldn't go without telling her mom. She woke up Krista and told her she and her friends were about to "sneak out and go to Walmart for Jujubes."[7] Her mom was fine with it. All Krista asked was that Emily call if they were out longer than an hour.

noting how it taught her teamwork, bolstered her self-esteem, and helped her cope with anxiety. "It taught me so much and helped me overcome so much. And I realized, okay, this is my job."[5] That sealed it—by the time she was in middle school, Emily was determined to become an actor.

When the budding performer turned 12, she decided it was not enough to pursue acting only after school and on weekends. She wanted more. Emily wanted to be homeschooled so the flexible schedule would give her more time to attend auditions during the day. All she had to do was convince her parents. So she grabbed some foam board, scissors, and glue and created a presentation.

The presentation worked. Her parents agreed to take her out of Cocopah Middle School. She did her schoolwork for her seventh and eighth grades at home. During those years, she went to auditions and performed in numerous plays at the Valley Youth Theatre. Emily also tried to branch out from theater. She even traveled to Los Angeles to audition for the preteen sketch comedy show *All That* on cable network Nickelodeon. She did not get the part, but she was not discouraged. She just kept on acting in whatever roles she could land.

After two years of homeschooling, Emily began her freshman year of high school at Catholic-affiliated Xavier College Preparatory. However, it wasn't long before she had concocted her next big plan. She was sitting in history class, lost in a daydream, when it hit her: if she wanted to be a serious actor, she had to move to Los Angeles.

IIIIIIIIII

Emily was only a freshman when she decided it was time to move to Hollywood.

Today, Emily is a movie icon because she followed a plan she dreamed up when she was 14.

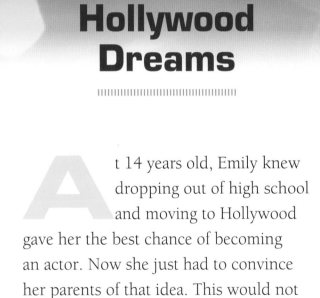

CHAPTER 3

Hollywood Dreams

||||||||||||||||||||||||||||||||||||||||||||||||

At 14 years old, Emily knew dropping out of high school and moving to Hollywood gave her the best chance of becoming an actor. Now she just had to convince her parents of that idea. This would not be an easy task, but Emily relied on the strategy that had worked in the past: it was time for another presentation.

This time, Emily ditched the foam board and glue in favor of computer software. She constructed her arguments on PowerPoint slides, setting her presentation to the less-than-subtle sound track of "Hollywood" by Madonna. She collected pictures, made charts, and decorated her slides with clip art. Anticipating her parents' counterargument that she should wait until she had finished high school, Emily also included photos of successful actors who had gotten early starts in the business, such as Sarah Jessica Parker. When Emily was satisfied with her work, she sat her parents down and served them popcorn. Then she showed them "Project Hollywood 2004."

Although the Stones did not immediately pack their bags, they were impressed by their daughter's ambition. They seriously considered her idea. However, they knew there was more to making it in Hollywood than just going to auditions. They felt Emily needed to be represented by an agent in order to make a move to Los Angeles worth it.

After several sessions with an acting coach, Emily was ready to audition for talent agencies. She had memorized a couple speeches from movies, including a comedic piece from the teen

Before signing with an agent, Emily's first step was to work with a local acting coach. Emily's dream was to act in movies someday, but her only experience was in theater. Therefore, she had developed an over-the-top acting style, with the big gestures and expressions necessary to perform on stage. Her coach helped her tone down her style so it would be better suited for movies, where more subtle techniques are needed. Emily was thankful for her coach's help. "She taught me to bring it down in teaspoons instead of buckets because, if you can imagine, I'm really hammy at heart," she later said.[1]

classic *Clueless*. Her performances impressed Savage Agency, which signed her and would officially represent her in Hollywood. The agency specialized in working with young talent. Emily's mother began looking for apartments in Los Angeles.

HOLLYWOOD HARDSHIPS

Emily turned 15 on November 6, 2003. Two months later, in January 2004, she left high school and flew with her mother to Los Angeles for pilot season. Between January and April, television studios in Hollywood are busy filming pilots, or trial episodes, with hopes that networks will pick up their shows. Emily and Krista settled into their new apartment, and Emily took online school courses while going out five or six times a week to audition for pilots.

Pilot season was no cakewalk. Each year during pilot season, thousands of actors, including children and teens with dreams of stardom, converge on Hollywood. Only a tiny percentage of them are actually cast. Emily learned firsthand the competition was fierce. To make things more difficult, Emily was picky about the roles she auditioned for. If a character description included adjectives such as *gorgeous* or *pretty*, she would refuse to audition for the part. Emily wanted to be cast as a comedian, not as a bimbo or a bombshell. She later said, "I just always thought I'd be a comedian. It was way more important to be funny or honest than to look a certain way."[2] Her manager soon took to deleting such words from the descriptions so she wouldn't rule out too many opportunities.

Unfortunately, Emily did not have to worry about choosing between funny and flirtatious roles.

She failed to land a single role. Once she had a solid string of rejections under her belt, her agency stopped sending her to auditions. Although Emily didn't give up on her dream, she couldn't help but be discouraged. This was not how she had envisioned her life in Hollywood.

> **"I went up for every single show on the Disney channel and auditioned to play the daughter on every single sitcom. I ended up getting none."[5]**
>
> *—EMMA STONE ON HER FIRST FEW MONTHS IN HOLLYWOOD*

With auditions no longer crowding her schedule, Emily spent her free hours looking for a job. She found one at a bakery specializing in dog treats. It was a fitting gig for an off-duty comedian. Emily learned how to bake "pup cakes and pup tarts" and other dog treats.[3] But it soon became clear baking for dogs was not Emily's calling. She laughs about it now. "I think three people called my specific cookies inedible to their dogs," she recalled. "I'm not a super-talented dog baker."[4]

Emily persevered with her side job as she watched and waited for her big break in acting.

EMILY ON TELEVISION

Finally, the opportunity arrived. Emily's mother spotted it. She was watching television one day when she saw a commercial advertising *In Search of the Partridge Family*, a reality show on the cable network VH1. Contestants on the reality show would compete to land a role in a remake of the 1970s sitcom *The Partridge Family*. Krista noted a resemblance between her daughter—who had recently dyed her naturally blonde hair brown—and Susan Dey, who had played Laurie Partridge on the original show. She encouraged Emily to attend the casting call. Emily reluctantly agreed.

To Emily's surprise, she secured a spot as one of eight contestants vying for the role of Laurie. During the televised competition, she sang, demonstrated her acting chops, and played up her resemblance to the original Laurie. Her efforts paid off—she won the competition. Winning meant she would play Laurie on the remake of the sitcom. It was her first television role.

A newly brunette Emily competed on a reality show casting actors for a *Partridge Family* remake.

Emily went on to film the pilot episode of *The New Partridge Family* in 2005. But in yet another disappointment, the rest of the series never made it on the air. The Partridge experience was not a total loss, however. Through connections to the show, Emily eventually met Doug Wald, who became her manager. The two would still be a team years later.

Emily needed a new name for her new career, which was slowly but surely taking off.

NEW NAMES, NEW OPPORTUNITIES

Under Wald's guidance, Emily would snag a few minor television spots. Emily registered with the Screen Actors Guild, a union representing actors. Since the name Emily Stone was already taken, she chose Riley Stone as her stage name. In 2005, she was credited as Riley Stone in an episode of the NBC drama *Medium*.

In 2006, she landed a guest role on an episode of the FOX sitcom *Malcolm in the Middle*. During the shoot, Emily realized her new name wasn't working: "Everyone kept on yelling, 'Riley!' and I didn't know who they were talking to."[6] She changed her stage name to something more familiar: Emma, the nickname her mother gave her.

That year, she also appeared on the HBO sitcom *Lucky Louie*, working with the experienced comedian Louis C. K. She was getting work, but it wasn't a lot, and it wasn't steady. She continued to audition for bigger, better parts. Her audition for *Heroes* may have ended with rejection, but it gave her new motivation. She was able to channel her feelings and land a regular role on the short-lived *Drive*.

Emily, now known as Emma Stone, saw more failure than success trying to break into television. But it meant she was open to opportunity, and her luck changed for good when she was cast in *Superbad*.

||||||||||

Stone had hilarious fun filming *Superbad* with costar Jonah Hill.

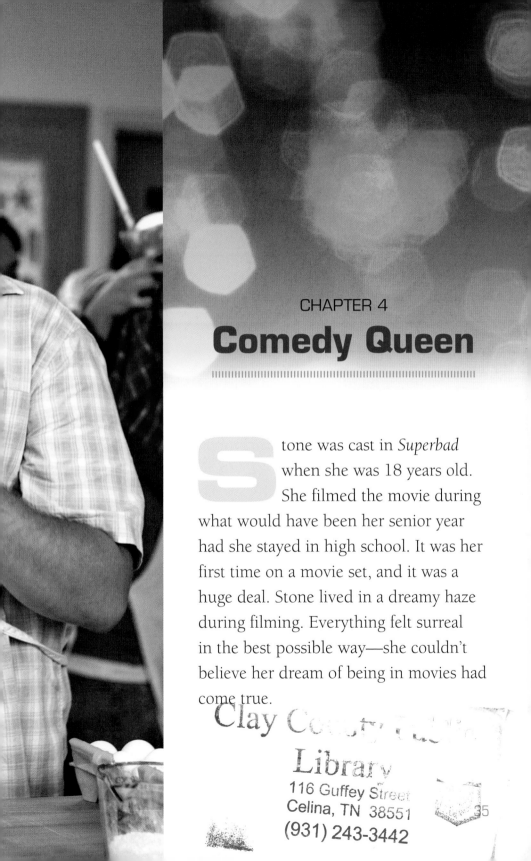

CHAPTER 4

Comedy Queen

||||||||||||||||||||||||||||||||||||||||||||||||||||||||||||||||||||||||||||||||||||||||||||||

Stone was cast in *Superbad* when she was 18 years old. She filmed the movie during what would have been her senior year had she stayed in high school. It was her first time on a movie set, and it was a huge deal. Stone lived in a dreamy haze during filming. Everything felt surreal in the best possible way—she couldn't believe her dream of being in movies had come true.

The best part of making *Superbad* was the sheer hilarity of it all. Stone fit right in with costars Jonah Hill and Michael Cera, plus a full cast of other comic actors. They were constantly goofing around and cracking jokes, both between and during takes. In fact, the hardest thing about filming was keeping a straight face through all the jokes. At the *Superbad* premiere, Stone admitted Hill and Cera were so funny they had her laughing in almost every take. She joked, "I think the takes they used in the movie were the only takes that I wasn't laughing in. So it's like 80 terrible takes, one good one, cool."[1]

"I thought that every movie was going to be like Superbad. I was like, 'Oh, this is fun. You can just make it up as you go.' But every movie is not like that."[2]

—EMMA STONE

Another thing that made *Superbad* exciting was that improv was encouraged. Every take was more hilarious than the last because the actors got to try something different every time. This made the task of keeping a straight face even harder, but Stone wouldn't have had it any other way. She was in her element, and she was having a blast. In many ways, *Superbad* was the perfect first movie experience for Stone. Those laughter-filled days on the set remain some of her fondest memories.

Superbad was released in the United States on August 17, 2007. It shot to number one at the box office, earning more than $30 million on its opening weekend.[3] Teens and critics alike enjoyed the raunchy yet surprisingly tender film. Although some found the film either too crude or too sweet, numerous critics praised producer Apatow's knack for conveying the complex psyches of teenage boys. Viewers also responded to the film's touchingly honest portrayal of the social discomforts of high school. *New York Times* reviewer Manohla Dargis wrote:

> *[The film] works because no matter how vulgar their words . . . these men and boys are good and decent and tender and true. They never take cruel or callous advantage. They call. They love. They marry.*[4]

Critics lavished most of the attention on the film's male stars: Hill, Cera, and Christopher Mintz-Plasse. However, audiences also connected with Stone and costar Martha MacIsaac. A *San Francisco Chronicle* review noted their characters had enough depth to transcend the stereotypes of typical teen-comedy crushes. "They're as quirky and interesting as the boys," the article said.[5]

THE ROCKER

Stone's charm in *Superbad* opened more doors for her in Hollywood. She was soon snapped up for roles in comedy films *The Rocker* and *The House Bunny*.

REDHEADS HAVE MORE FUN

After dying her hair red for *Superbad*, Stone found people didn't want her to go back to her natural blonde. She chatted about her hair dilemma on *Late Night with Jimmy Fallon*, saying, "Everything I auditioned for after [*Superbad*] they were like, 'Let's keep it red! How about a different shade of red?' . . . I was like, 'Maybe we could be blonde?' and they were like, 'Or red!'"[6] *Superbad* producer Apatow, who was in the audience, yelled out, "I'm sorry. I still like it better red."[7]

Increasingly a favorite in comedies, Stone next appeared as a bass guitarist in *The Rocker*.

The Rocker tells the story of aging, has-been drummer Robert "Fish" Fishman. He gets to relive his past days of fame when his nephew asks him to fill in as the drummer in a high school rock band. Craziness ensues when Fish takes his teenage bandmates on tour. Stone was cast as Amelia, the bassist in the band.

In preparation for her part, Stone took bass guitar lessons. She learned to play every song in the movie. Another challenging aspect was that Amelia doesn't so much as crack a smile until the end of the movie. Laughter-loving Stone had a hard time keeping it serious, especially while working with funny costars Rainn Wilson and Teddy Geiger.

But she could give her smile free rein once they wrapped for the day. The film was shot mostly at night, so there were plenty of late-night hangout sessions where the cast listened to music together or caught a movie. Something else was happening off camera too: a romance was developing between Stone and Geiger.

TEDDY GEIGER

Teddy Geiger is perhaps better known as a singer and songwriter than as an actor. He and Stone first met years before *The Rocker*, when they were both competing for roles on VH1's *In Search of the Partridge Family* in 2004. Geiger was a finalist for the role of Keith Partridge. However, the two didn't spend any time together back then. Similar to Stone, Geiger launched his career from the reality show performances. He signed with Columbia Records and released his first album, *Underage Thinking*, in 2006. His hit single "For You I Will (Confidence)" made it into the Top 40 on the *Billboard* charts. Two years later, he and Stone had a new chance to get to know each other on the set of *The Rocker*.

Despite the fun Stone and the others had filming, *The Rocker* was a box office flop. Released on August 20, 2008, it brought in less than $3 million on its opening weekend.[8] Critics offered mixed reviews. Many felt it hit its mark as a lighthearted comedy but didn't stand out enough to be a success. Stone's *The House Bunny*, released two days later, would fare better.

THE HOUSE BUNNY

The House Bunny is about a young woman, played by Anna Faris, who lives in the Playboy Mansion but then gets kicked out. She ends up becoming the housemother of a college sorority made up of social rejects. She helps them gain confidence in themselves. Stone was cast as Natalie, the nerdy president of the socially awkward sorority.

Filming *The House Bunny* was a bit different from filming *Superbad* and *The Rocker*, but in a good way. Instead of working mostly with men, Stone joined a cast of hilarious women. Along with Faris, the group included Rumer Willis, Kat Dennings, and *American Idol* star Katharine McPhee. The group had a lot of fun together.

Faris and Stone fed off each other's performances while filming *The House Bunny*.

Stone was thrilled she was once again able to show off her improv skills as she had in *Superbad*. She especially enjoyed improvising with Faris and playing off her antics.

The House Bunny arrived in theaters two days after the release of *The Rocker*. Unlike *The Rocker*, *The House Bunny* hit number one the day it opened. By the end of the opening weekend, it had grossed more than $14.5 million.[9] Critics raved about Faris's perfect performance as the naïve but gorgeous blonde. But once again, they had mixed reviews for the movie itself. Some felt it was good-enough fluff, while others panned its lack of originality.

Despite the lukewarm reviews, Stone got a small amount of positive exposure from the film. One reviewer said Stone "finds the right note of believable nerdy awkwardness" and that "she and Faris make a good team."[10]

By the end of 2008, Stone was on cloud nine. She had given impressive performances in three comedy films. Offers for other parts were rolling in. Now 21, Stone knew she had made the right decision in coming to Hollywood as a teen. She was well on her way to making it big.

||||||||||

AZTEC PARTY SCENE ||||||||||||||||||||||||||||||||||||||||||||||||||||||||||||||||||||

Stone had an amazing time shooting *The House Bunny*, but one scene was even more fabulous than the rest. In the movie, Faris's character comes up with the idea of throwing an Aztec-themed party to help her sorority girls gain popularity. Stone's character, Natalie, is to be "sacrificed" at the party.

The elaborate set for the Aztec party included a three-story model of a volcano filled with gelatin "lava." To film the scene, Stone, dressed in a sparkly white bikini and headdress, had to step into the lava and pretend to melt. She found the gelatin sticky and a little disgusting, but the fun of riding down the side of the volcano on a waterslide and dancing around in her Aztec costume more than made up for it.

After making a name for herself
in several comedies, Stone
was ready to branch out.

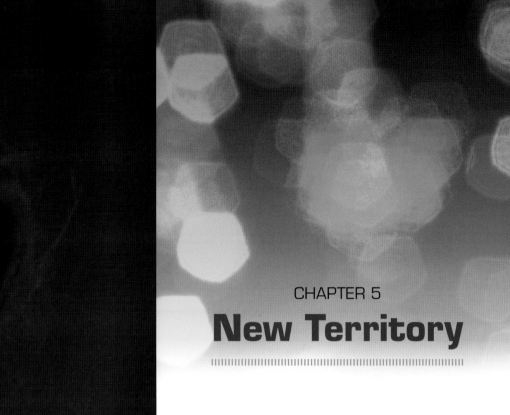

CHAPTER 5

New Territory

||||||||||||||||||||||||||||||||||||||||||||||||||||||||||||||||||||||||||||||||||||||||||||||||||

A fter *The House Bunny* came even more success for Stone. She made her next appearance in the romantic comedy *Ghosts of Girlfriends Past*. The movie stars Matthew McConaughey as Connor Mead. With frizzy hair and braces, Stone's character is the ghost of Mead's first girlfriend. The movie was received as mediocre at best, but Stone did not disappoint as a hilarious blast from the 1980s.

Stone was happy to learn from a more experienced actor such as McConaughey, and she really enjoyed working with director Mark Waters. He gave his actors space to try out new lines and ideas in almost every scene. But after having completed so many comedies in such a short time, Stone was exhausted. Her creativity was drained. She hoped the right role would come along to replenish her.

PAPER MAN

As Stone was recovering from her marathon of comedies, she received a script for *Paper Man*. It was a much darker, more serious film than any she had acted in before. The premise was compelling: a young woman and a middle-aged man, both with imaginary friends, forge an unexpected, complex friendship while he tries to write his second novel. Stone felt particularly connected to the character Abby.

Paper Man was new emotional territory for Stone, and she had to work hard to get the part. After her initial audition, she was called back three times. Each time, she faced a lengthy audition with surprises thrown at her. It was a nerve-racking process, but ultimately, Stone was cast as Abby. When she and costar Jeff Daniels came together over breakfast to get a feel for their chemistry, the pair hit it off immediately. Everything was coming together. Shooting would begin in Montauk, New York, in November 2008.

But in October, just before Stone began filming, the actress got a phone call that shattered her world. It was her mother calling from Arizona to say she had been diagnosed with an aggressive form of breast cancer. She was only 48 years old.

TRIPLE NEGATIVE BREAST CANCER

Stone's mother was diagnosed with triple negative breast cancer, a relatively rare form of the disease. Triple negative tumors lack the three types of receptors that most commonly cause breast cancer growth: estrogen, progesterone, and human epidermal growth factor receptor 2. That means triple negative breast cancer does not respond to the most common treatments for breast cancer, such as hormone therapy. Chemotherapy is often an effective treatment. However, triple negative breast cancer is more difficult to treat than other forms of breast cancer, and it is also more likely to recur.

Stone did whatever she could to support her mother, Krista, during her courageous battle with cancer.

Stone had always been incredibly close to her mother, and the news was shocking and terrifying.

Somehow, Stone was able to keep it together for Krista. "I was oddly stoic," she said.[1] She assured Krista they would fight the cancer and beat it. When she had to leave for Montauk, she was thousands of miles from her mom, who would undergo months of chemotherapy and a double mastectomy. Stone flew to Arizona whenever she had a break from filming.

In addition to Stone's tireless worry about her mother, she found the filming experience for *Paper Man* intense at times. One of the major challenges was the frigid temperature in Montauk in November. Stone and the other actors often struggled to keep from shivering. Stone also had to do a scene where she submerged herself in the ocean when it was below freezing outside.

But perhaps the biggest challenge for Stone was getting out of her comfort zone as a comedian. Her character, Abby, has some deeply emotional scenes, and Stone didn't feel she was doing them justice. She explained in an interview, "I wasn't emotionally getting to someplace I felt I needed to be." Daniels noticed her frustration and told her, "Emma, they're going to add sad violins."[2] She realized then the audience's reaction to a scene depends on a lot more than the actor's performance. The other elements—the music, the lighting, the camera angles—boosted her own performance. It lifted some of the pressure she had put on herself.

The film was an important learning experience for Stone. It really taught her what it meant to be an actor. She became so in touch with her character she felt a sense of loss when filming was over. "[Abby is] alive in me in every way," Stone said.[3]

Stone formed strong friendships with Daniels and her other costars, including Ryan Reynolds and Kieran Culkin. By that time, Stone and Geiger had drifted apart as a couple. She connected in a special way with Culkin, whose character is Abby's imaginary friend. Stone believes strongly in protecting the privacy of those close to her, so she let rumors fly without confirming or denying an offscreen romance. But when she and Culkin were spotted holding hands while strolling, it became obvious they were a couple.

Paper Man was released in theaters on June 15, 2009. Although most viewers and critics were put off by the film's metaphorical, oddball plot, Daniels's and Stone's performances were almost universally deemed stunning. *New York Times* reviewer Stephen Holden said of Stone's character: "Abby is an appealing lost soul with a redeeming streak of spunkiness, and when Ms. Stone is on screen, her performance bypasses the pretensions of a movie constructed on abstractions."[6]

Paper Man did terribly at the box office, but Stone considered the film a success in other ways. Her acting skills had deepened through the layers and subtleties of playing a role like Abby. She also felt it was her truest, most convincing performance.

ZOMBIELAND

The next script Stone fell in love with was another complete change of pace for her. It was

Zombieland—part action movie, part horror fest, part comedy. Stone snagged an audition. As with *Paper Man*, Stone outshone all the other auditioning actresses even though she had no experience with the genre. It helped that she auditioned with Jesse Eisenberg, who would win a part in the movie as well. They had easy chemistry doing improv together. Ultimately, Stone was cast in the role of Wichita, a con artist with a troubled past and a little sister in tow.

Eisenberg played a young man trying to find his family, and Abigail Breslin was cast as Wichita's little sister. Woody Harrelson, playing a Twinkie-loving zombie killer, was the fourth member of their band of postapocalyptic survivors. In the film, the quartet have both hilarious and terrifying encounters with diseased, fast-moving zombies on their way to an amusement park.

The small cast became close as they filmed in Atlanta, Georgia. Stone and Breslin formed a particularly special bond, like sisters. Stone said they were so inseparable they were called "Emmigail."[7] Harrelson took Stone to visit his friend Paul McCartney, a rock legend formerly of the Beatles, and they chatted over veggie burgers.

As for Eisenberg, he simply cracked Stone up. She said he was "maybe the funniest person I've ever met. . . . I've never met anybody like him."[8]

Filming, for the most part, was a blast for Stone. A cautious person by nature, she loved stepping outside herself to play a fiery, take-no-prisoners character. Pretending to kill zombies was pretty awesome, but Stone had the most fun during a scene in which the band of survivors completely trashes a store, breaking everything in sight.

Some parts of filming proved to be more challenging, though. For instance, Stone injured herself while running during a scene. She ended up limping around the set, trying to mask her pain when she had to do an action scene. Another

ZOMBIE PURISTS

While most zombie fans couldn't get enough of *Zombieland*, some were less than thrilled with the film's interpretation of the creatures. So-called zombie purists believe zombies must be slow moving and dead by definition. Rather, the *Zombieland* zombies are very fast on their feet, and they are still alive, infected with a mutated strain of mad cow disease. Aware of the rule-breaking twist, Stone said, "We were going to be excommunicated from the zombie community by a fair number of zombie fans."[9]

Playing a zombie-killing con artist was a fun departure for Stone.

difficulty was trying to eat while "zombies" dripping with bloody, gory makeup wandered the set at lunchtime. There were also moments, especially in the middle of the night, when the thought of being chased by zombies became legitimately scary. She said of the actors playing zombies, "You're like, one of them is going to snap! One of them is going to snap at any moment!"[10]

The challenges were all worth it in the end. *Zombieland* was an instant hit when it came out in theaters on October 2, 2009. It earned more than $60 million in 17 days, making it one of the highest-grossing zombie movies ever.[11] Audiences loved it, including vast numbers of avid zombie fans. Even critics tended to enjoy the film's comic take on zombies. Most important, the film's success set Stone up for her biggest role yet.

||||||||||

In *Easy A*, Stone defined herself as a headlining actress with sass and smarts.

CHAPTER 6

Stardom and Saturday Night

||||||||||||||||||||||||||||||||||||||||||||||||||||||||||||||||||||||||||||||||||||||||||

T he fall of 2009 was a bit of a whirlwind for Stone. She was busy promoting *Zombieland*, and she was also doing her best to support her mother, who was struggling through chemotherapy. Even with so much going on at the time, Stone got the urge to move away from Los Angeles.

She noticed how practically everyone in Los Angeles was in the film industry.

And nearly every conversation she overheard was about a film. She didn't feel she could lead a normal life in the Hollywood bubble. She relocated to Greenwich Village in New York City. After settling in her new home, it wasn't long before the 21-year-old actress was back at work. This time, she would take on the pressure of a leading role.

EASY A

Stone read the script for the teen comedy *Easy A* and immediately loved it. Loosely inspired by Nathaniel Hawthorne's classic book *The Scarlet Letter*, the story follows high school student Olive Penderghast, a good girl pretending to be a bad girl. Olive lies to a friend about losing her virginity, and rumors circulate throughout the school. Instead of trying to stop the rumors, Olive finds a way to use them for her own gain.

Stone loved that Olive was a fleshed-out, relatable character funny in her own right, rather than just a supporting role to a funny male character. Stone knew she would be perfect for the role, and she went after it with her usual gusto. She set up a meeting with director Will Gluck. Gluck was already a fan of hers. "As soon as I heard that Emma Stone wanted to do [*Easy A*], I was very excited," he said.[1]

> "Will [Gluck] told me he wasn't looking for someone to become Olive. He was looking for someone that was Olive, because Olive becomes whoever is playing her. I understood that there was no becoming this girl. You either were or weren't Olive. I'm so thankful that they gave me the chance."[2]
>
> —EMMA STONE

When auditions opened, Stone wanted to be the first in the casting room. She did well, then just as she was about to leave, Gluck threw a curveball at her. Since Olive narrates much of the movie via Webcam, Gluck gave Stone an assignment to make a Webcam video of herself performing a monologue from the film. She chose the opening monologue and immediately started when she got home. Stone recorded her one-minute performance over and over again for hours. She wanted to make it absolutely perfect. Finally, a friend convinced her to just send it.

Stone was eager to film herself doing one of Olive's Webcam monologues.

Stone's monologue was the first—and only—one in Gluck's inbox. All the other actresses vying for the part were waiting while their agents called with questions about the Webcam assignment. It wasn't a hard decision for Gluck. He knew Stone had to be Olive Penderghast. "I took the disc with [Stone's Webcam] scene to the head of the studio and said, 'This is the girl.' She was, by far, always my first choice," Gluck said.[3]

Stone was elated she had landed her first starring role. For the first time, she would be playing the main character—not just a supporting or bit role. But soon she started feeling the pressure that came with a leading role. She was afraid of failing to bring to life the Olive she loved in the script. She was concerned Olive would be unlikeable if she played her the wrong way. As Olive, Stone had to walk a fine line—being sneaky, deceptive, and sarcastic while still making the audience love her.

Filming was intense. Stone rarely had a break from the camera. The pressure made her increasingly, almost unbearably, anxious. She could hardly sleep, and she also developed horrible acne. Makeup wasn't enough to hide it. Instead, the film editors had to do some special-effect video airbrushing to make her face appear flawless on film.

But there were some lighter moments during production, too. Stone got to revive her musical theater skills during a song and dance complete with a feather boa. She also really connected with Patricia Clarkson and Stanley Tucci, the actors who played Olive's parents. They were hilarious, and the characters reminded Stone of her own parents' open-minded willingness to let their daughter be who she was.

When filming ended, Stone felt a huge relief. "It felt like a house had been lifted off me," she said.[4] The weight of the role, plus the weight of her mother's battle with cancer, had been heavy. "I felt a great deal of pressure making that movie, because in my personal life at the time, too, things were just . . . it was like a hurricane."[5]

Easy A came out on September 17, 2010. The film did well both at the box office and with critics.

MTV MOVIE AWARDS

Stone's stress and anxiety during *Easy A* paid off. Her performance earned her an MTV movie award in June 2011—her first award for acting. She was shocked when she beat out Russell Brand, Zach Galifianakis, Ashton Kutcher, and Adam Sandler to win Best Comedic Performance. During her charmingly humble acceptance speech, she said, "I'm pretty sure all the people in this category are much, much funnier than me, but thank you for voting, and this really made my night and my week and my year."[6]

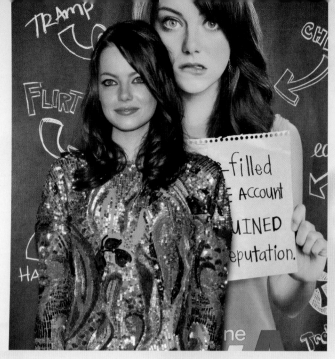

After all the pressure, Stone's *Easy A* performance lifted her to another level as a Hollywood star.

Legendary reviewer Roger Ebert sang Stone's praises, saying,

> [Easy A is] *a funny, engaging comedy that takes the familiar but underrated Emma Stone and makes her, I believe, a star. Until actors are matched to the right role, we can never quite see them clearly.*[7]

Aside from the movie being a hit, Stone had even more to be happy about that fall. Her mother had come through the bulk of her cancer treatments and was officially cancer-free. The pair

To celebrate the victory over cancer, Stone and Krista decided to get matching tattoos. Their favorite song was "Blackbird," a Beatles' song written by Paul McCartney. Having met McCartney while filming *Zombieland*, Stone wrote a letter to the rock icon. She asked if he would draw a pair of blackbird feet for their tattoo design. McCartney agreed and sent the drawing. Stone and her mother had the design inked on their wrists.

planned to get matching tattoos to commemorate the occasion. Also, Stone's relationship with Culkin still seemed to be going strong. The couple created a buzz with more public appearances. Best of all, Stone was invited to host *SNL*—one of her lifelong dreams—in October.

|||||||||||||||||||||||||||||||||||||||||||||||||

LIVE FROM NEW YORK!

Stone had dreamed of being on *SNL* since her mother first introduced her to the show. Each week, the show features a celebrity host who performs an opening monologue and appears in sketches with the regular cast. Stone had always maintained that hosting *SNL* was her only true career goal and wildest wish. "If that ever happened," she had said in a 2009 interview, "then I wouldn't have anything to dream about."[8] When Stone found out the show's producers wanted her to host, she was beside herself with excitement. "I cried on the floor for a while," she said. "It's like becoming president or something."[9]

In the week before the show, Stone rehearsed and hung out with many of the *SNL* cast members she idolized, including Kristen Wiig. The live performance aired on October 23, 2010. Stone's opening monologue poked fun at how her characters are frequently the love interests of nerdy boys. As the show continued, the actress appeared in a number of sketches. In a sketch with an overenthusiastic Wiig, Stone's character is a homeowner who is unimpressed with the news she has won a home makeover. Stone also participated in a ridiculous French dance-off, perfected her Lindsay Lohan impression, and rapped about breaking her arm. All in all, it was a wonderful and hilarious night.

GOLDEN GIRL

Just when Stone thought 2010 could not get any better, it did. The morning of December 14, she woke to a phone call from Wald, her manager. At first, she thought something terrible had happened. "My manager called me sounding very upset, which is what you think when someone calls you at 5:30 in the morning," she said. "Then I realized it was excitement and he wasn't upset."[10] The excitement was that Stone's performance in *Easy A* had earned her a Golden Globe nomination for Best Performance by an Actress in a Motion Picture—Comedy or Musical. It came as a huge surprise that she was up for the same award as Angelina Jolie, Anne Hathaway, and Julianne Moore.

The night of the Golden Globe Awards show was wonderful too, even though Stone didn't win in the end. She glowed in a sleek peach-colored dress by Calvin Klein. In a comedy bit for the award presentation, Robert Downey Jr. flirted with her and all the other nominees in her category. It was a star-studded night, and Stone shined with the best.

||||||||||

Nominated for her first Golden Globe Award, Stone created a stir on the red carpet.

Stone's career was on fire, and the flame would only grow with new roles in a new year.

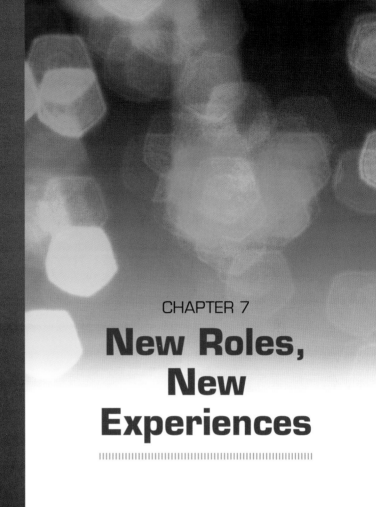

CHAPTER 7

New Roles, New Experiences

||||||||||||||||||||||||||||||||||||||||||||||||||||||||||||||||||||||||||||||

Stone was on top of the world in 2010, but she was not one to rest on her laurels. She wanted to keep pushing her limits and pushing her talent in new areas. It seemed 2011 was going to be another big year for Stone.

To kick off things on a fun note, Stone was at work again in another comedy soon after *Easy A*. This time, she made a brief appearance in *Friends with Benefits*, which stars Justin Timberlake and Mila Kunis. Stone's character is a crazy girlfriend who breaks up with Timberlake's character outside a John Mayer concert.

With such a small role, Stone was on the set for only one night. But the scene didn't flow effortlessly. At first, Stone took her character's crazy description to an extreme. "I screamed at Justin Timberlake over and over again until I lost my voice," she said.[1] Finally Gluck—who also directed her in *Easy A*—suggested she was taking the scene in the wrong direction. He had her tone it way down. By the time the sun came up, though, the scene wrapped. Screaming or not, Stone had a lot of fun breaking up with heartthrob Timberlake.

CRAZY, STUPID, LOVE

A week after *Friends with Benefits* released in July 2011, Stone had another new romantic comedy hitting theaters. In *Crazy, Stupid, Love*,

Stone had come a long way since refusing to audition for "pretty" roles as a teenager. By the 2010s, people everywhere admired her for her talent as well as her charming looks. Stone was asked to do a cover shoot for the August 2011 issue of fashion magazine *Vanity Fair*. Doing magazine photo shoots wasn't something Stone was used to or particularly comfortable with, but she agreed to it. She traveled to the luxurious Caribbean island of Saint Barthélemy for the shoot with French fashion photographer Patrick Demarchelier. Stone had to wear a bikini for the shoot, which she was modest about. "I usually wear a one-piece," she told the magazine.[2] The photos turned out beautifully. But Stone was still glad when the next issue came out and she didn't have to see her image everywhere.

she played Hannah, the love interest of Ryan Gosling's character.

When she first read the script, Stone was impressed by how surprising yet realistic it was. She scored an audition, and she decided to just have fun with the character. Hannah was supposed to be a little bit crazy, especially when intoxicated. The audition scenes were from some of those tipsy moments. Stone ran with it. She was convincing enough to be called back to read some scenes with costar Gosling. Stone and Gosling had an obvious connection right from the start. "I immediately felt a kinship with him," she said.[3] The two also practiced a fancy lift for a dance scene, similar to a move from the classic movie *Dirty Dancing*.

Filming was exciting because Stone was surrounded by talented actors, including Julianne Moore and the hilarious Steve Carell. She and Gosling worked closely together and did improv in several scenes. For one scene, the director let the actors perform unscripted all day. They were encouraged to just talk and make each other laugh. The result was a bedroom scene that felt real and intimate but was funny at the same time.

One scene that proved too real was the one with the *Dirty Dancing*–style lift. Stone had been practicing with Gosling since their audition, but on the day of filming, Stone couldn't go through with it. She had a panic attack she believed stemmed from a moment in her childhood gymnastics class when she fell off the parallel bars and broke both arms. As soon as Gosling lifted her above his head, Stone started screaming. Then she kicked him in the throat and clung to his head "like a spider monkey," she said.[4] The director had to have a

While working together on *Crazy, Stupid, Love*, Stone and Gosling had a fun dynamic on and off the screen.

stunt double fill in for her at the last minute, but the scene came together well in the end.

The rest of the movie came together well, too. Released July 29, 2011, the film was somewhat successful at the box office, earning almost $20 million during its opening weekend.[5] Critics had mostly positive things to say about the film, especially about the performances. *Los Angeles Times* reviewer Betsy Sharkey had high praise for Stone:

Her beauty is built on a nontraditional look that includes a lot of inner strength. She's spicy instead of being just a sweet tart, and she's always as smart as she is funny. All that plays off Gosling's nuanced performance just about perfectly.[6]

THE HELP

The increasingly in-demand Stone had yet another film coming out the summer of 2011. *The Help* was a serious, dramatic role. As if that weren't enough pressure, the film was based on her mother's favorite book. The story follows Skeeter Phelan, a young white journalist who grew up in Mississippi in the 1960s. Skeeter finds her journalism voice by sympathizing with and writing about the struggles of the African-American maids who largely raised her.

Stone landed the role of Skeeter without a single audition. Instead, she was handpicked for the part. She participated in a series of meetings with Tate Taylor, the director, and Kathryn Stockett, the author of the book. They knew she was right for the role. "No one else could be playing Skeeter but Emma Stone," said Taylor.

As Skeeter Phelan, Stone brought to life a character so many readers loved from *The Help*.

"It was just so obvious."[7] Stone immediately accepted. Her mother was almost as excited as she was. "My mom's never cried when I've gotten a part before, and she lost her mind when we found out about Skeeter," said Stone.[8]

The Help was filmed on location in Mississippi. Stone and costars Viola Davis, Octavia Spencer, and Bryce Dallas Howard got to know each other. Mississippi was hot and sticky, and they could feel the weight of the state's history during the civil rights era. But it helped them understand their characters and produce a film that felt authentic. The cast also enjoyed a taste of Southern hospitality with Taylor's mom's home cooking.

For Stone, one of the most challenging aspects of filming *The Help* was perfecting her Mississippi dialect. Having to pay so much attention to her accent made it more difficult to act and react naturally. It was almost as though she were performing in a foreign language. Stone also felt the heavy responsibility of representing a beloved literary character as well as portraying an emotionally charged era. But she found a way to get past the pressure and just give the best performance she could. Luckily, once Stone got into costume and put on her curly wig, she felt more at home in her character.

The movie was well received, although many accused it of shying away from the more unsavory aspects of racial tension. The lead actors' performances, especially Spencer's, made the film memorable, and Stone brought Skeeter's intelligence and well-intentioned naïveté to life. At the box office, *The Help* earned more than $26 million in its first weekend in August 2011 and remained the highest-grossing film in the country for several weeks.[9]

"Viola [Davis] keeps saying this movie should be called *The Big Responsibility* instead of *The Help*, because there were so many groups of people that you want to do right by. You want to do right by Southerners and the African-American community and the readers of the book and the people that grew up with domestics and the people who worked as domestics. There are a million different groups that you're trying to please and satisfy."[10]

—*EMMA STONE ON THE PRESSURES OF FILMING THE HELP*

In the midst of this busy 2011 with three summer movies coming out, Stone experienced some turmoil in her personal life. She and longtime boyfriend Culkin were having difficulties, and they broke up that summer. But Stone soon had other films—and romantic prospects—on the horizon.

In *The Amazing Spider-Man*, her first blockbuster, Stone caught the attention of a web slinger.

CHAPTER 8

Blockbuster

||||||||||||||||||||||||||||||||||||||||||||||||||||||||||||||||||||||||

By 2011, Stone had been steadily working up to her biggest project yet. Movie studio Sony Pictures had worked with Stone on a few films, including *Easy A*. Now Sony invited her to audition for the role of Gwen Stacy, Spider-Man's first love, in a reimagining of the Spider-Man superhero story. Stone did some research on the story and was excited to try out for the part.

British actor Andrew Garfield had already been cast as Spider-Man and alter ego Peter Parker. The most important aspect of Stone's audition was the chemistry between her and Garfield. From the earliest moments, it was clear there was something special between them. During their screen test, they had a natural connection and were able to easily improvise scenes and dialogue. Both had quick wit and high energy, and something just clicked.

> "She came in, and she was like a shot of espresso. She was like being bathed in sunlight. She's incredibly energetic and enthusiastic, and she had this sense of play and fun, which was incredibly exciting."[1]
>
> —ANDREW GARFIELD ON AUDITIONING WITH EMMA STONE FOR THE AMAZING SPIDER-MAN

After seeing the screen test, director Mark Webb felt Stone was the obvious choice for the part. The filmmakers offered Stone the role, but she almost didn't accept it. She worried *The*

Amazing Spider-Man would be too big. She was afraid so much exposure would make it difficult to live a normal life afterward. In the end, though, Stone realized she couldn't base her decision on such assumptions. She loved the story and wanted to be part of it, so she dyed her hair back to blonde and took on the role.

THE AMAZING SPIDER-MAN

Filming took place primarily in Los Angeles, although some scenes were shot on location in New York City. For the most part, Stone didn't feel she was filming a major blockbuster. Webb gave the cast the freedom to experiment with scenes until they felt right. He also scaled down the crew while filming the romantic scenes so Stone and Garfield could be in a more intimate setting. All in all, it felt like filming any other movie—with a couple exceptions. One was the stunts. Stone's role wasn't nearly as stunt heavy as Garfield's, but she still had to don a harness and do some swinging. Stone recalled:

> *When we shot the swinging sequence, that was crazy. When you're strapped into a harness*

swinging 20 feet [6 meters] above the ground, you really step outside of yourself a bit.[2]

Stone also felt the extreme pressure of playing such a well-known and well-loved comic book character. Her anxiety returned, and she began feeling out of control. Fortunately, she found a way to channel those feelings into a cathartic hobby: she took up baking. It made her feel in control because if she followed a recipe, she knew what would come out of the oven. With lots of anxiety to bake away, she said, "There were stacks of things in the kitchen that nobody could possibly go through. . . . I was overbaking."[3]

With several other Spider-Man films in existence, Webb had a vision for a more realistic, more sarcastic, grittier version of Spider-Man

"Andrew is one of the most giving actors I've ever worked with. If I needed to get to a place of love or sadness in a scene, he'd leave messages on my phone to replay, or slip in lines off camera for a different reaction than what was scripted. He gave me so much to react to."[4]

—EMMA STONE ON WORKING WITH ANDREW GARFIELD

With so much publicity surrounding the film, Stone and Garfield had a hard time keeping their relationship secret.

and his world. Stone and Garfield had the task of making their relationship feel like an awkward but powerful high school love rather than a fairy-tale romance. The chemistry that had sparked during their screen test transferred easily onto film. And when Stone and Garfield both found themselves single, they transferred that chemistry offscreen, too.

As usual, Stone tried to keep the relationship private. It was difficult, though, with paparazzi lurking, rumors buzzing, and a busy publicity schedule. Even though *The Amazing Spider-Man* wasn't scheduled for release until 2012, the couple

COMIC-CON

had their first publicity event at Comic-Con, the annual comic book convention, in July 2011. Stone loved meeting the Spider-Man superfans there. Still, the two knew they had a long year ahead of them, promoting their film in the public eye while trying to keep their relationship out of it.

STANDING UP TO CANCER

In the year leading up to the Spider-Man release, Stone had a few other important things on her agenda. She got involved in a campaign for Stand Up To Cancer, an organization that funds research for all types of cancer. Stone filmed some promotional videos for the organization. In one, she appeared as the character Princess Leia in a *Star Wars* spoof. The entire *Amazing Spider-Man* cast became active in supporting the organization after Laura Ziskin, one of the film's producers and also a Stand Up to Cancer cofounder, lost her battle to breast cancer in June 2011.

Then in August 2011, Revlon announced Stone would be one of the new faces of the cosmetics company. Stone was eager to become one of Revlon's ambassadors because she would also be involved in the company's charity endeavors. Stone's ad campaigns helped raise money for a number of charitable organizations devoted to women's health issues, including breast cancer. After her mother's close call with the disease, breast cancer research was a cause especially close to Stone's heart.

SNL, TAKE TWO

On November 12, 2011, Stone was thrilled to host *SNL* for the second time. Her opening monologue centered on her role as Stacy in *The Amazing Spider-Man*. She had some hilarious but not very nice words to say about Mary Jane Watson, another of Spider-Man's love interests from the previous Spider-Man movie franchise. Garfield made a surprise appearance at the end of the monologue.

Once again, Stone was featured in a number of sketches. One of the funniest had her sobbing along with coworkers while listening to pop singer Adele's tearjerker "Someone Like You." Stone held her own in each role and remained a favorite host for the show.

LOVE AND SPIDER-MAN

After much fanfare and even more interviews, *The Amazing Spider-Man* was released on July 3, 2012. The film was number one at the box office during opening weekend and raked in more than $62 million. Overall, the movie earned just over $262 million in the United States alone.[6]

By the time the movie came out, there were plans for a sequel. *The Amazing Spider-Man 2* was scheduled for release in 2014. With a strong career and a strong relationship, Stone was ready for whatever came next.

Stone's performance as Gwen Stacy gave *The Amazing Spider-Man* a realistic love story.

Stone's career keeps gaining
more and more momentum.

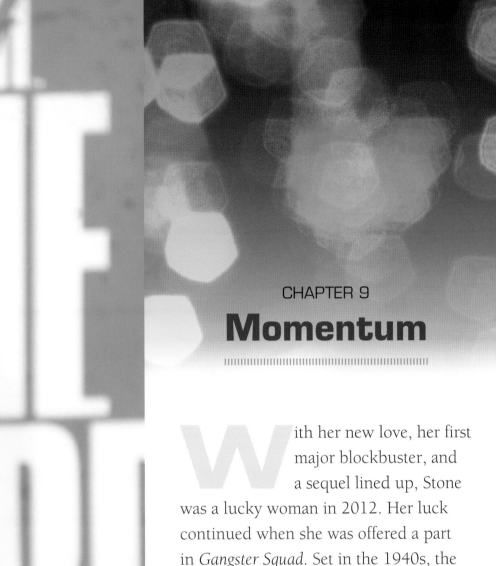

CHAPTER 9

Momentum

||||||||||||||||||||||||||||||||||||||||||||||||||||||||||||||||||||||

With her new love, her first major blockbuster, and a sequel lined up, Stone was a lucky woman in 2012. Her luck continued when she was offered a part in *Gangster Squad*. Set in the 1940s, the movie is about real-life gangster Mickey Cohen. It gave Stone another chance to work with director Ruben Fleischer, who had directed *Zombieland*. She was also thrilled the cast included Gosling, with whom she had become friends while filming *Crazy, Stupid, Love*. It also included widely respected actor Sean Penn.

Stone agreed to play Grace Faraday, a glamorous redhead desperate to become a Hollywood star. Grace gets involved with Cohen and his gang, then begins a secret affair with Gosling's character, one of the cops after Cohen. A lot of the fun was being able to experience the 1940s through the film's fabulous sets, costumes, and makeup. Stone had to wear a corset during filming, but otherwise she enjoyed the glamorous gowns and full hair and makeup treatment of a Hollywood starlet from that era.

Although *Gangster Squad* is based on a true story, Stone's character is fictional. This decreased some of the pressure of having to provide an authentic representation of history. However, other challenges cropped up, including keeping a straight face with Gosling around. The two were so used to working in a comedic context it proved difficult to stay serious at times. Also, Stone had some difficulties with dialect, similar to her challenges with *The Help*. This time, she had hired a vocal coach to help her cultivate a mid-Atlantic

In *Gangster Squad*, Stone was treated to the fashion and style of 1940s Hollywood.

accent, but the director wanted the dialect to be subtler than what she had rehearsed.

Working with Penn was another interesting part of the process. Unfortunately, Stone didn't have many scenes where she was interacting with Penn's character. But she was awestruck just watching his complete transformation into character. One time he even did a dead-on impression of another character, completely transforming himself in an instant. She described, "He turned into this terrifying guy with this tiny voice who was talking about his cat. I was like . . . 'This guy is touched by something.'"[1]

Gangster Squad was released in theaters on January 11, 2013. Its star-studded cast and rich visuals attracted audiences, but ultimately the film was disappointing. Many felt the writing was lackluster and the plot was dull. In addition, there was a sense of discontinuity. A movie theater shootout scene had to be replaced after a tragic shooting occurred at a movie theater in Aurora, Colorado. Despite the mediocre reviews, Stone enjoyed being part of the film and felt she had learned a lot from her costars.

AURORA SHOOTING

Gangster Squad was originally set to release in the fall of 2012. However, a national tragedy spurred a change in plans. On July 20, 2012, a 24-year-old man opened fire in an Aurora, Colorado, movie theater during a showing of *The Dark Knight Rises*. He killed 12 and wounded 58.[2] A sequence from the original version of *Gangster Squad* involved a shooting in a movie theater, but the filmmakers decided it was no longer appropriate to include that scene. The release date was pushed back to allow extra filming for a different scene that would be less upsetting.

THE CROODS

Next, Stone had another chance to try something new as well as reunite with a former castmate. She signed on to be the voice of the cavegirl Eep in the animated movie *The Croods*. Ryan Reynolds, with whom she had worked on *Paper Man*, voiced Guy, Eep's caveboy love interest.

Stone loved being able to really let loose with her character and not have to worry about going over the top. She said,

> *It was really fun to get to be a human cartoon. It's like my dream come true to go as big as possible and not have anyone tell you to tone it down.*[3]

Released on March 22, 2013, the film was a family hit at the box office. It opened at number one, earning more than $43 million during its opening weekend.[4] Overall, critics gave positive reviews. For Stone, it was a fun way to broaden her experience as an actor.

Stone and Garfield revived their onscreen chemistry as they filmed *The Amazing Spider-Man 2*.

NEW PROJECTS

As Stone was promoting *The Croods*, production for *The Amazing Spider-Man 2* was already underway in New York. She and Garfield were spotted filming a high school graduation scene in addition to a daring flying-through-the-air rescue. Filming was completed in June 2013, with a lot of postproduction and publicity work still ahead before the expected release date of May 2, 2014. Sony also announced there would be at least two more sequels to *The Amazing Spider-Man*.

In the spring of 2013, Stone was also filming another movie, *Birdman*. The comedy stars Michael

Keaton as an actor past his prime, and Stone plays his character's daughter. *Birdman* was slated for release in 2014.

|||||||||||||||||||||||||||||||||||||||||||||||||

GOING STRONG

Everything in Stone's life seemed to be gaining momentum. In mid-2013, her relationship with Garfield was apparently still going strong, and the actress's career had not slowed down for a moment.

Stone feels extremely lucky about her career, but she knows how important it is to not get caught up in her success. She stated,

> I can't worry about what I'll do if this or that happens, otherwise I'd go crazy. If you'd asked me five years ago what I thought I'd be doing, it wouldn't be all this. I would never have dared dream this for myself.[5]

Stone's down-to-earth attitude, playful sense of humor, and lightning-quick intelligence have set her apart from her peers in the industry. The world will just have to wait and see where her career takes her next.

||||||||||

TIMELINE

1988
Emily Jean Stone is born on November 6.

2004
In January, Stone moves to Los Angeles, California, with her mother.

2005
Stone lands her first television role as Laurie Partridge in *The New Partridge Family*, but the show never makes it past the first episode.

2008
Stone appears in *The House Bunny*, released on August 22.

2008
In October, Stone's mother is diagnosed with breast cancer.

2009
Paper Man opens on June 15.

2006

2007

2008

Stone auditions for the role of Claire Bennet on the show *Heroes* and is devastated when Hayden Panettiere is cast instead.

On August 17, Stone makes her film debut in the teen comedy *Superbad*.

Stone's second comedy, *The Rocker*, is released on August 20.

2009

2009

2010

On October 2, Stone's action comedy *Zombieland* comes out in theaters.

Stone moves from Los Angeles to New York City in the fall.

Stone stars in *Easy A*.

TIMELINE

2010

On October 23, Stone hosts *Saturday Night Live* for the first time.

2010

Stone finds out on December 14 that she is a nominee for a Golden Globe Award.

2011

In June, Stone wins an MTV movie award for Best Comedic Performance for *Easy A*.

2011

Stone becomes a new face and ambassador for Revlon.

2011

On November 12, Stone hosts *SNL* for the second time.

2012

Stone stars in the blockbuster film *The Amazing Spider-Man*, which is released on July 3.

2011	2011	2011

Stone is cast opposite Ryan Gosling in *Crazy, Stupid, Love,* released July 29.

Stone's first film adaptation, *The Help*, comes out in August.

Stone appears on the August cover of fashion magazine *Vanity Fair*.

2013	2013	2013

Gangster Squad opens in theaters on January 11.

Stone plays the voice of Eep in animated film *The Croods*, released on March 22.

Stone completes filming for *The Amazing Spider-Man 2* in June.

FULL NAME

Emily Jean Stone

DATE OF BIRTH

November 6, 1988

PLACE OF BIRTH

Scottsdale, Arizona

SELECTED FILMS AND TELEVISION APPEARANCES

The New Partridge Family (2005), *Medium* (2005), *Malcolm in the Middle* (2006), *Lucky Louie* (2006), *Drive* (2007), *Superbad* (2007), *The House Bunny* (2008), *Paper Man* (2009), *Zombieland* (2009), *Easy A* (2010), *Crazy, Stupid, Love* (2011), *The Help* (2011), *The Amazing Spider-Man* (2012), *Gangster Squad* (2013), *The Croods* (2013)

SELECTED AWARDS

- Golden Globe nominee for Best Performance by an Actress in a Motion Picture—Comedy or Musical for *Easy A* (2011)
- MTV movie award winner for Best Comedic Performance for *Easy A* (2011)

PHILANTHROPY

Since her mother's breast cancer diagnosis in 2008, Stone has actively supported causes devoted to breast cancer research and helping cancer patients. She has contributed to campaigns for Stand Up to Cancer and a number of women's health organizations supported by cosmetics company Revlon.

"I just always thought I'd be a comedian. It was way more important to be funny or honest than to look a certain way."

—EMMA STONE

GLOSSARY

agent—A person who protects the business interests of an actor.

blockbuster—A particularly large or extravagant movie.

box office—The place where tickets are sold at a theater; a term used to describe the amount of income a movie makes with ticket sales.

cathartic—Emotionally purifying.

chart—A weekly listing of songs or films in order of popularity or sales.

chemotherapy—The use of chemicals to treat cancer.

double mastectomy—The surgical removal of all or part of both breasts.

improvisation—The art of inventing a performance on the spot, without prior rehearsal.

monologue—A speech performed by a single actor.

paparazzi—Freelance photographers whose job it is to follow celebrities with hopes of getting exclusive pictures.

pilot—An episode of a television show made as a sample before producing a longer series.

postapocalyptic—Taking place after a terrible disaster.

postproduction—The finishing work, such as editing, that is done after the filming of a movie, video, or television show.

sitcom—A television show about a group of characters involved in different humorous situations.

sketch—A comic variety act having a single scene.

stoic—Showing no emotion.

ADDITIONAL RESOURCES

SELECTED BIBLIOGRAPHY

Crowe, Cameron. "Emma Stone." *Interview Magazine.*
Interview Magazine, n.d. Web. 3 Sept. 2013.

Heller, Nathan. "Emma Stone Makes Her *Vogue* Cover
Debut in the July Issue." *Vogue.* Condé Nast, 2012.
Web. 3 Sept. 2013.

Wolfe, Alexandra. "Hollywood Is Her Oyster." *Vanity Fair.*
Condé Nast, Aug. 2011. Web. 3 Sept. 2013.

FURTHER READINGS

Lee, Stan, ed. *The Ultimate Spider-Man.* New York: Berkley,
1994. Print.

Shales, Tom. *Live from New York: An Uncensored History of
Saturday Night Live.* Boston: Back Bay, 2003. Print.

WEB SITES

To learn more about Emma Stone, visit ABDO Publishing
Company online at **www.abdopublishing.com**. Web sites
about Emma Stone are featured on our Book Links page.
These links are routinely monitored and updated to provide
the most current information available.

PLACES TO VISIT

Sony Pictures Studios
10202 Washington Boulevard
Culver City, CA 90232
310-244-4000
http://www.sonypicturesstudios.com
Tour the movie studio where Stone filmed parts of *The Amazing Spider-Man*. Daily tours reveal the filmmaking process and let visitors explore sets and soundstages.

Valley Youth Theatre
525 North First Street
Phoenix, AZ 85004
602-253-8188
http://www.vyt.com
Take in a show at the youth theater where Emma Stone got her start in show business.

SOURCE NOTES

CHAPTER 1. UP FROM ROCK BOTTOM

1. Alexandra Wolfe. "Hollywood Is Her Oyster." *Vanity Fair.* Condé Nast, Aug. 2011. Web. 3 Sept. 2013.

2. "Emma Stone Biography." *People.* Time, 2013. Web. 3 Sept. 2013.

3. Alexandra Wolfe. "Hollywood Is Her Oyster." *Vanity Fair.* Condé Nast, Aug. 2011. Web. 3 Sept. 2013.

4. Jessica Kiang. "Interview: Emma Stone Talks Comedy, 'The Croods' And Cameron Crowe; Scores Off the Charts on Likability." *Airing News.* Airing News, 24 Feb. 2013. Web. 3 Sept. 2013.

5. "Video: *Superbad*—Christopher Mintz-Plasse Interview." *About.com Hollywood Movies.* About.com, 2013. Web. 3 Sept. 2013.

6. "Rising Star: Emma Stone." *Access Hollywood.* NBC Universal, 4 June 2008. Web. 3 Sept. 2013.

7. Andrea Mandell. "Emma Stone Is Summer's Hot Ticket." *USA Today.* USA Today, 27 July 2011. Web. 3 Sept. 2013

CHAPTER 2. ASPIRING STAR

1. Marlow Stern. "Emma Stone, Revealed." *Gale Biography in Context.* Newsweek, 9 July 2012. Web. 30 Aug.

2. Jillian Gordon. "Emma Stone: The Coolest Chick We Know." *Saturday Night.* Saturday Night Magazine, n.d. Web. 3 Sept. 2013.

3. Nathan Heller. "Emma Stone Makes Her *Vogue* Cover Debut in the July Issue." *Vogue.* Condé Nast, 2012. Web. 3 Sept. 2013.

4. Cameron Crowe. "Emma Stone." *Interview Magazine.* Interview Magazine, n.d. Web. 3 Sept. 2013.

5. Steven Whitty. "Emma Stone Interview: Down-to-Earth Actress Is All Color and Charm." *NJ.com.* NJ.com, 31 July 2011. Web. 3 Sept. 2013.

6. Alexandra Wolfe. "Hollywood Is Her Oyster." *Vanity Fair.* Condé Nast, Aug. 2011. Web. 3 Sept. 2013.

7. Ibid.

CHAPTER 3. HOLLYWOOD DREAMS

1. Alexandra Wolfe. "Hollywood Is Her Oyster." *Vanity Fair.* Condé Nast, Aug. 2011. Web. 3 Sept. 2013.

2. Lynn Hirschberg. "Emma Stone." *W.* Condé Nast, Jan. 2011. Web. 3 Sept. 2013.

3. Alexa Chung. "The Crazy Cool of Emma Stone." *Vogue UK.* Condé Nast, 10 July 2012. Web. 19 June 2013.

4. Alexandra Wolfe. "Hollywood Is Her Oyster." *Vanity Fair.* Condé Nast, Aug. 2011. Web. 3 Sept. 2013.

5. "Emma Stone Biography." *People.* Time, 2013. Web. 3 Sept. 2013.

6. Cameron Crowe. "Emma Stone." *Interview Magazine.* Interview Magazine, n.d. Web. 3 Sept. 2013.

CHAPTER 4. COMEDY QUEEN

1. "Video: *Superbad*—Christopher Mintz-Plasse Interview." *About.com Hollywood Movies.* About.com, 2013. Web. 3 Sept. 2013.

2. Cameron Crowe. "Emma Stone." *Interview Magazine.* Interview Magazine, n.d. Web. 3 Sept. 2013.

3. "*Superbad.*" *Box Office Mojo.* IMDd.com, n.d. Web. 3 Sept. 2013.

4. Manohla Dargis. "For Three Virgins, the Path to Sunrise Is Paved with Excess." *New York Times.* New York Times, 17 Aug. 2007. Web. 3 Sept. 2013.

5. Mick LaSalle. "Review: Teen on a Mission to Buy Booze in 'Superbad.'" *San Francisco Chronicle.* Hearst Communications, 16 Aug. 2007. Web. 3 Sept. 2013.

6. "Late Night: Judd Apatow Cameo on Emma Stone Interview." *Vulture.* New York Media, 2011. Web. 3 Sept. 2013.

7. Ibid.

8. "*The Rocker.*" *Box Office Mojo.* IMDd.com, n.d. Web. 3 Sept. 2013.

9. "*The House Bunny.*" *Box Office Mojo.* IMDd.com, n.d. Web. 3 Sept. 2013.

10. "*The House Bunny* Movie Review." *ContactMusic.com.* ContactMusic.com, 2008. Web. 3 Sept. 2013.

CHAPTER 5. NEW TERRITORY

1. Kristen Mascia. "Emma Stone: My Mom's Cancer Diagnosis 'Was Terrifying.'" *People.* Time, 22 May 2013. Web. 3 Sept. 2013.

2. Alexandra Wolfe. "Hollywood Is Her Oyster." *Vanity Fair.* Condé Nast, Aug. 2011. Web. 3 Sept. 2013.

3. Carla Hay. "Jeff Daniels and Emma Stone Write the Book on Quirky Friendships in 'Paper Man.'" *Examiner.com.* Clarity Digital Group, 21 Apr. 2010. Web. 3 Sept. 2013.

4. Cameron Crowe. "Emma Stone." *Interview Magazine.* Interview Magazine, n.d. Web. 3 Sept. 2013.

5. Ibid.

6. Stephen Holden. "Triangle: Man, Wife, and Friend (Imaginary)." *New York Times.* New York Times, 22 Apr. 2010. Web. 3 Sept. 2013.

7. "Interview with Emma Stone for *Zombieland.*" *YouTube.* YouTube, 30 Sept. 2009. Web. 3 Sept. 2013.

8. Ibid.

9. "Lynn Hirschberg's Screen Tests: Emma Stone." *YouTube.* YouTube, 14 Jan. 2011. Web. 3 Sept. 2013.

10. "Video: *Zombieland*—Emma Stone Interview, Comic Con." *About.com.* About.com, 2009. Web. 3 Sept. 2013.

11. Brandon Gray. "Weekend Report: 'Wild Things' Roars, 'Citizen,' 'Activity' Thrill." *Box Office Mojo.* IMDd.com, 19 Oct. 2009. Web. 3 Sept. 2013.

CHAPTER 6. STARDOM AND *SATURDAY NIGHT*

1. "*Easy A* Production Notes." *Sony Pictures.* Sony Pictures, 2010. Web. 3 Sept. 2013.

2. *Easy A* Production Notes." *Cinema Review.* Cinema Review, 2013. Web. 3 Sept. 2013.

3. "*Easy A* Production Notes." *Sony Pictures.* Sony Pictures, 2010. Web. 3 Sept. 2013.

4. Cameron Crowe. "Emma Stone." *Interview Magazine.* Interview Magazine, n.d. Web. 3 Sept. 2013.

5. Ibid.

6. "MTV Movie Awards 2011 Best Comedic Performance." *YouTube.* YouTube, 17 June 2011. Web. 3 Sept. 2013.

7. Roger Ebert. "*Easy A.*" *RogerEbert.com.* Ebert Digital, 15 Sept. 2010. Web. 3 Sept. 2013.

8. Ben Barna. "'*Zombieland*'s' Emma Stone Dreams of *SNL* and Mexican Food." *BlackBook.* BlackBook, 2 Oct. 2009. Web. 30 Aug. 2013.

9. "Emma Stone: It's My 'Biggest Dream' to Host 'Saturday Night Live.'" *Access Hollywood.* Hulu, 2010. Web. 3 Sept. 2013.

10. Eric Ditzian. "Emma Stone Says Golden Globe Nomination Made Her Year 'Truly Bizarre.'" *MTV.* Viacom, 14 Dec. 2010. Web. 3 Sept. 2013.

CHAPTER 7. NEW ROLES, NEW EXPERIENCES

1. Cameron Crowe. "Emma Stone." *Interview Magazine.* Interview Magazine, n.d. Web. 3 Sept. 2013.

2. Alexandra Wolfe. "Hollywood Is Her Oyster." *Vanity Fair.* Condé Nast, Aug. 2011. Web. 3 Sept. 2013.

3. Cameron Crowe. "Emma Stone." *Interview Magazine.* Interview Magazine, n.d. Web. 3 Sept. 2013.

4. Matt Goldberg. "Emma Stone Interview *Crazy Stupid Love.*" *Collider.com.* TopLingo, 2011. Web. 3 Sept. 2013.

5. "*Crazy, Stupid, Love.*" *Box Office Mojo.* IMDd.com, n. d. Web. 3 Sept. 2013.

6. Betsy Sharkey. "Movie Review: 'Crazy, Stupid, Love.'" *Los Angeles Times.* Los Angeles Times, 29 July 2011. Web. 3 Sept. 2013.

7. "*The Help* Production Notes." *DreamWorks Pictures and Participant Media.* DreamWorks Pictures and Participant Media, 2011. Web. 3 Sept. 2013.

8. "Emma Stone Feels the Pressure." *ABC News.* ABC News, 14 July 2011. Web. 3 Sept. 2013.

9. "*The Help.*" *Box Office Mojo.* IMDd.com, n. d. Web. 3 Sept. 2013.

10. Kyle Ryan. "Interview: Emma Stone." *A.V. Club.* The Onion, 9 Aug. 2011. Web. 3 Sept. 2013.

CHAPTER 8. BLOCKBUSTER

1. Terri Schwartz. "Andrew Garfield and Emma Stone Had 'Fireworks' During 'Spider-Man' Audition." *MTV*. Viacom International, 7 Nov. 2012. Web. 3 Sept. 2013.

2. "Emma Stone on 'The Amazing Spider-Man,' Andrew Garfield, and More." *Daily Beast*. Newsweek/Daily Beast, 26 June 2012. Web. 3 Sept. 2013.

3. Nathan Heller. "Emma Stone Makes Her *Vogue* Cover Debut in the July Issue." *Vogue*. Condé Nast, 2012. Web. 3 Sept. 2013.

4. Beth Anne Macaluso. "Andrew Garfield: How I Fell for Emma Stone." *US Weekly*. US Weekly, 12 June 2012. Web. 3 Sept. 2013.

5. "About Comic-Con International." *Comic-Con International: San Diego*. San Diego Comic Convention, 2013. Web. 3 Sept. 2013.

6. "The Amazing Spider-Man." *Box Office Mojo*. IMDd.com, n. d. Web. 3 Sept. 2013.

CHAPTER 9. MOMENTUM

1. Cameron Crowe. "Emma Stone." *Interview Magazine*. Interview Magazine, n.d. Web. 3 Sept. 2013.

2. "Aurora Theater Shooting." *DenverPost.com*. Denver Post, 2013. Web. 3 Sept. 2013.

3. "Emma Stone: *The Croods* Is a 'Dream Come True.'" *Access Hollywood*. NBC Universal, 2011. Web. 3 Sept. 2013.

4. "*The Croods*." *Box Office Mojo*. IMDd.com, n. d. Web. 3 Sept. 2013.

5. Simon Button. "Emma Stone: Success Is Fleeting So I'm Not Going to Sell My Soul." *Express*. Express, 5 Mar. 2012. Web. 3 Sept. 2013.

INDEX

ABOUT THE AUTHOR

Lisa Owings has a degree in English and creative writing from the University of Minnesota. She has written and edited a wide variety of educational books for young people. Owings lives in Andover, Minnesota, with her husband and a small menagerie of pets.